D0340582

In the Land of Pain

Daudet and his wife, Julia, at Champrosay, *c.* 1892.

In the Land of Pain

ALPHONSE DAUDET

edited and translated by
Julian Barnes

Alfred A. Knopf New York 2002

THIS IS A BORZOI BOOK
PUBLISHED BY ALFRED A. KNOPF

Translation, introduction, and notes copyright © 2002 by
Julian Barnes

All rights reserved under International and Pan-American
Copyright Conventions. Published in the United States by
Alfred A. Knopf, a division of Random House, Inc.,
New York. Distributed by Random House, Inc., New York.

www.aaknopf.com

This translation originally published in Great Britain by
Jonathan Cape, London, in 2002. This work is based
on the unpublished notes of Alphonse Daudet.

Knopf, Borzoi Books, and the colophon are registered
trademarks of Random House, Inc.

ISBN 0-375-41485-1
LCCN 2002114929

Manufactured in the United States of America
First American Edition

Introduction

In 1883 Turgenev had an operation in Paris for the removal of a neuroma in the lower abdomen. The doctors gave him ether rather than chloroform, and he was conscious throughout the intervention. Afterwards, he was visited by his friend Alphonse Daudet, with whom he had often dined in the company of Flaubert, Edmond de Goncourt, Zola and others. 'During the operation,' Turgenev told him, 'I thought about our dinners and tried to find the right words to convey exactly the sense of the steel slicing through my skin and entering my body . . . It was like a knife cutting into a banana.' Goncourt, recording this anecdote, commented, 'Our old friend Turgenev is a true man of letters.'

How is it best to write about illness, and dying, and death? Despite Turgenev's impeccable example, pain is normally the enemy of the descriptive powers. When it became his turn to suffer, Daudet discovered that pain, like passion, drives out language. Words come 'only when everything is over, when things have calmed down. They refer only to memory, and are either powerless or untruthful.' The prospect of dying may, or may not, concentrate the mind and encourage a final truthfulness; may or may not include the useful *aide-mémoire* of your life passing before your eyes; but it is unlikely to make you a better writer. Modest or jaunty, wise or vainglorious, literary or journalistic, you will write no better, no worse. And your literary temperament may, or may not, prove suited to this new thematic challenge. When Harold Brodkey's heroic — and, it seemed, heroically self-deceiving — account of his own dying was published in the *New Yorker*, I congratulated the magazine's editor for 'leaving it all in', by which I meant the evidence of Brodkey's impressive egomania. 'You should have seen what we took out,' she replied wryly.

Alphonse Daudet (1840–97) is a substantially forgotten writer nowadays. Novelist, playwright, journalist, he is viewed as a sunny humorist and clear stylist, creator in *Lettres de mon moulin* and *Tartarin de Tarascon* of an agreeable if partial Provence. He is offered to students of French as a nursery slope or climbing wall: practise on this. But in his day he was not only highly successful (and very rich); he also ate at the top literary table. Dickens called him 'my little brother in France'; Henry James, who translated Daudet's novel *Port-Tarascon*, called him 'a great little novelist'; Goncourt '*mon petit Daudet*'. As may be deduced, he was short of stature. He was also kind, generous and sociable, a passionate observer and an unstoppable talker. These qualities transfer into his fiction. He was, in various descriptions (all of them from Henry James), 'the happiest novelist of his day', 'beyond comparison the most *charming* story-teller of the day', 'an observer not perhaps of the deepest things of life, but of the whole realm of the immediate, the expressive, the actual'. As these assessments, laudatory yet limiting, imply, Daudet was the sort of writer — hard-working, honourable, popular — whose fame and relevance are largely used up in his own lifetime. The twenty-volume collected edition of 1929–32 seemed to have said (more than) it all. In Anglo-Saxon countries the surname Daudet nowadays refers as often to Alphonse's elder son Léon, the highly gifted polemicist who followed an intransigent path to ultra-nationalism, royalism and anti-semitism; who was co-founder, with Charles Maurras, of *L'Action française*.

If Daudet dined in the highest company, he was also a member of a less enviable nineteenth-century French club: that of literary syphilitics. Here again, he is somewhat over-shadowed: the Big Three were Baudelaire, Flaubert and Maupassant. Daudet probably ranks fourth, equal with Jules de Goncourt, Edmond's younger brother. He could at least claim that the syphilis he acquired, shortly after his arrival in Paris at the age of seventeen, came from a classier, indeed more literary, source than theirs. He caught it from a *lectrice de la cour*, a woman employed to read aloud at the Imperial court. She was, he assured Goncourt, a lady 'from the top drawer'.

After its initial declaration, and treatment with mercury, the disease lay dormant; Daudet worked, published, became famous, married (in 1867), had three children. He also continued an active, carefree, careless sex life. From the time he lost his virginity at the age of twelve, he had always been 'a real villain' in matters of sex, he once confessed; he slept with many of his friends' mistresses; about ten times a year he felt the need for the sort of '*ordure*' he could not ask his wife to permit. Drink for him led inevitably to debauchery (and contrition, and forgiveness); but then so did many other things. In 1884 he had an operation for a hydrocele. Having a grossly swollen testicle painfully drained (and then drained again when the first operation didn't work) would probably make most men sleep in their trousers for weeks; Daudet's reaction was to go straight out in search of sex. In 1889 he reported to Edmond de Goncourt a dream in which he was caught up in the Last Judgement and defending himself against a sentence of 3,500 years in hell for 'the crime of sensuality'.

When his syphilis reached the tertiary stage, it initially reasserted itself as 'rheumatism', severe fatigue and haemorrhages. By the early 1880s, however, it became increasingly clear that Daudet was suffering from the form of neurosyphilis known as tabes dorsalis: literally, wasting of the back. Its chief manifestations in his case were locomotor ataxia (the progressive inability to control one's movements) and, eventually, paralysis. In 1885 J-M Charcot, the greatest neurologist of the day, declared him 'lost'; Daudet was to live another twelve years, in increasing pain and debility, after hearing this death sentence. He saw the finest specialists, who sent him to the finest thermal establishments, where he took the waters and mud-baths. He tried all the latest treatments, no matter how violent and outlandish. Charcot recommended the Seyre suspension, in which the patient was hung up, some of the time by the jaw alone, for several minutes. It caused excruciating pain and did little good. David Gruby, doctor to the artistic (whose client list included Chopin, Liszt, George Sand, Dumas *père et fils* and Heine), suggested an esoteric diet. The day began with a soup made from a large variety of grains and vegetables; its visceral consequences were so volcanic that Daudet said death was preferable. In his last years he tried the Brown-Séquard treatment, a course of extremely painful injections with an elixir extracted from guinea pigs (one day the injector told Daudet that they had run out of guinea pigs, and were using extract of bulls' testicles instead). At first the treatment — which Zola also took, in an attempt to increase his sexual powers — seemed beneficial, even miraculous; then, swiftly, it didn't.

None of these doctors was a quack (Charles Edward Brown-Séquard, for instance, was professor of physiology and neuropathology at Harvard, and the first to show that epilepsy could be produced experimentally in guinea pigs);

each was trying to outwit a then invincible disease. Daudet, like many other sufferers, came to rely on large quantities of palliative drugs: in particular chloral, bromide and morphine. At different times his wife, son Léon and father-in-law were all giving him morphine injections. In March 1887 Léon gave him two injections in a row but refused a third; so Daudet went to his father-in-law who gave him two more. (The father-in-law was also a morphine addict; the son preferred laudanum.) Increasingly, he injected himself, no easy task when you are both ataxic and extremely myopic. In June 1891 he reported giving himself five injections in a row; this despite the fact that the previous October he had been unable to find any place left on his body to inject.

His response, both personal and literary, to his condition was admirable. 'Courage . . . means not scaring others,' Larkin wrote. Numerous witnesses attest to Daudet's exemplary behaviour. His last secretary, André Ebner, remembered Daudet sitting with a friend one morning, eyes closed, barely able to speak, martyred by pain. The door-knob gently turned, but before Mme Daudet could enter, her husband was on his feet, the colour back in his cheeks, laughter in his eye, his voice filled with reassurance about his condition. When the door closed again, Daudet collapsed back into his chair. 'Suffering is nothing,' he murmured. 'It's all a matter of preventing those you love from suffering.' This is a difficult, correct (and nowadays unfashionable) position. It led

Daudet to familiarity with all the ironies and paradoxes of long-term illness. Surrounded by those you love, and unwilling to inflict pain on them, you deliberately talk down your suffering, and thus deprive yourself of the comfort you crave. Next, you discover that your pain, while always new to you, quickly becomes repetitive and banal to your intimates: you fear becoming a symptoms bore. Meanwhile, the anticipation of indignities to come – and the terror of disgusting those you love – makes suicide not just tempting but logical; the catch is that those you love have already insisted that you live, if only for them.

Daudet's other response to his suffering was to write about it. He began taking notes, but the book he had in mind presented all kinds of problems. It shouldn't be a novel, it should be an honest confession; but how could he write an honest confession – which would include the 'sexual desires and longings for death that illness provokes' – when he was a married man? By 1888 he thinks he has solved the question of form. Autobiography is still ruled out, even if published posthumously: he doesn't want to leave 'a testament of complaint against my family'. But: 'Listen,' he tells Goncourt, 'it begins like this. The terrace of the hotel at Lamalou. Someone says, "He's dead!" Then a character sketch of myself, done by myself. Then the dead man's servant slips his notebook into my hand. You see, like that, it's not me. I'm not even married in the book, and that will give me a chapter to make the comparison between suffering in the midst of a family and suffering alone. This notebook allows me a fragmented form, so that I can talk about everything, without the need for transition.' There is special pleading, even desperation, in this proposed solution. In any case, Mme Daudet persuaded her husband of the project's unfeasibility. Her argument, according to their son Lucien, was that such a work would inevitably appear to be the concluding act of a literary career, and might well prevent Daudet from writing anything thereafter. Such reasoning was either genuine or exceedingly clever.

There is no evidence that Daudet ever started serious work on his book about Pain. But he continued taking notes, talked about the project, and even answered journalists' questions about its progress (this not long before his death). One thing he always knew was what he was going to call it: *La Doulou*, the Provençal word for *douleur*, pain. Goncourt thought the title 'abominable', but expected the result to be 'superb' because Daudet would have lived the book, even 'lived it too much'. What was eventually published as *La Doulou* in 1930 consists of fifty or so pages of notes on his symptoms and sufferings, his fears and reflections, and on the strange social life of patients at shower-bath and spa. But they are superb, and Daudet was right to feel himself well suited to this subject. He was 'a true man of letters' in the Turgenev sense. He always had been. When he was sixteen, his brother Henri had died, at which moment their father gave vent to a great howl of 'He's dead! He's dead!' Daudet was aware, he wrote later, of his own bifurcated response to the scene: 'My first Me was in tears, but my second Me was thinking, "What a terrific cry! It would be really good in the theatre!" ' From that point on he was '*homo duplex, homo duplex!*' 'I've often thought about this dreadful duality. This terrible second Me is always there, sitting in a chair watching, while the first Me stands up, performs actions, lives, suffers, struggles away. This second Me that I've never been able to get drunk, or make cry, or put to sleep. And how much he sees into things! And how he mocks!'

'The artist, to my way of thinking, is a monstrosity, something outside nature,' Flaubert wrote. Daudet certainly feels monstrous to himself in these lines, almost revolted by the condition of being a writer. Some writers succeed in putting the second Me to sleep, or getting it drunk; others are less constantly aware of its presence; still others have an active and effective second Me, yet an unworthy or tedious first one. Graham Greene's line about the writer needing a chip of ice in the heart is true; but if there's too much ice, or the chip cools down the heart, the second Me has nothing – or nothing interesting – to observe.

Daudet had the cold eye and the warm, suffering heart. He also had a sense of the ordinary. What happens around illness may be dramatic, even heroic; but illness itself is ordinary, day-to-day, boring. Turgenev compared himself to a banana; Daudet, when caught in a frenzied bout of loco-motor ataxia, his leg hopelessly out of control, reminded himself of a knife-grinder. (The comparison may be lost on some modern readers: until a few decades ago itinerant knife-grinders would trundle the streets with circular stones mounted on wheeled carriers; to make his stone revolve at a speed sufficient to sharpen your knives and shears, the grinder would pump frantically up and down on a pedal.) The image is exact, unheroic, and taken from daily life.

La Doulou, though organized, and with a certain inevitable plot-progression, remains a collection of notes; but this isn't necessarily a disadvantage. Notes seem an appropriate form in which to deal with one's dying. They imply the time, and the suffering, which elapses between each being made: here is a decade or so of torment reduced to fifty pages. Notes minimize the danger of Brodkeyism; also, the temptation to disguise, to make too much art of it all. Daudet was a realist who frequently wrote close to his own life. Here — in what Léon Daudet called a 'terrible and implacable breviary' — he is writing close to his own death.

He had no illusions about immortality. He and Goncourt had discussed the matter in 1891. Goncourt outlined his own beliefs: that death means complete anni-hilation, that we are mere ephemeral gatherings of matter, and that even if there were a God, expecting Him to provide a second existence for every single one of us would be laying far too great a bookkeeping job on Him. Daudet agreed with all this, and then recounted to Goncourt a dream he had once had, in which he was walking through a field of broom. All around him there was the soft background noise of seed-pods exploding. Our lives, he had concluded, amount to no more than this: just a quiet crackle of popping pods.

Julian Barnes

I

Μαθήματα – Παθήματα

Μαθήματα – Παθήματα.* – The elemental truths. – Pain.

'What are you doing at the moment?'
'I'm in pain.'

In my cubicle at the shower-baths, in front of the mirror: what emaciation! I've suddenly turned into a funny little old man.

I've vaulted from forty-five to sixty-five. Twenty years I haven't experienced.

The shower-baths – cubicle neighbours: the little Spaniard, the Russian general. Shrunken bodies, feverish eyes, scrawny shoulders.

Monsieur B——'s passion for absinthe.

Stock-exchange men coming at the end of the day.

* A variant of a common Greek tag: 'Suffering is instructive.'

At the back, the fencing-hall. Ayat with his provosts. Choderlos, who fences with a stick.

Savate.* Boxing. Monsieur de V—— (two showers a day for years) lifts some weights, then goes and weighs himself at the back.

The to-and-fro of the invalid carriage.

The steam-rooms.

Monsieur B——, sometimes in the invalid carriage, plump, white-fleshed, with every appearance of health; other times carried, supported, scarcely able to walk.

Shower noises, ringing voices, the metallic click of foils from the back room. The deep sadness this causes me — the physical life of which I am no longer capable.[†]

Poor night-birds, beating against the walls, blind despite their open eyes.

Torture walking back from the baths via the Champs-Elysées. Six o'clock, a beautiful evening, rows of seats laid out.

* A French version of kick-boxing; both a gymnastic exercise and a sport.
[†] In April 1885, while 'tottering around his billiard table', Daudet told Edmond de Goncourt that he had tried to fence with one of the seconds-in-command at the hydrotherapy establishment, but had fallen over. 'How is it that I, whose mind has kept all the youth, the vigour and the drive of my best years, have ended up with a body like a wet rag?'

Concentration on walking straight. Fear of an attack: shooting pains that either nail me to the spot, or twist me around so that my foot pumps up and down like a knife-grinder's. Even so it's the most convenient route, and the least painful for my feet: I have to keep walking.*

Coming back from the baths with X——, who's gone in the head. On the way I comfort him, I 'rub him down', just for the simple human pleasure of keeping myself warm.

'The illness of a neighbour is always a comfort and may even be a cure.' A proverb from the Midi, the land of the sick.

'The ship has fouled' is the nautical phrase. I need some such term to describe the crisis I find myself in . . .

The ship has fouled. Will it ever pull free?

My father's death. The wake. The burial. What I saw, what I remember, what haunts me.†

---

* Daudet to Goncourt (*Journal*, 19 June 1884): 'I have to keep walking to wear out my pain.'
† Vincent Daudet had died in 1875.

Memory of my first visit to Dr Guyon in the rue Ville-l'Evêque. He probed me: some tenseness in the bladder, the prostate a little sensitive. In a word, nothing. But that *nothing* was the start of *everything:* the Invasion.*

Warning signs going back a long way. Strange aches; great flames of pain furrowing my body, cutting it to pieces, lighting it up.

Dream of the boat's keel, so sharp, so painful.†

A burning feeling in the eyes. The hideous pain from light reflected in a window.

Also, from that time onwards, pins and needles in the feet, burning feelings, hyper-sensitivity.

At first, a heightened awareness of sound: the noise of the shovel, tongs near the hearth, the screech of doorbells; the ticking watch, a spider's web on which work begins at four in the morning.

---

* Félix Guyon (1831–1920), the great urologist. 'False urinary symptoms' are typical of the onset of tabes dorsalis.

† 'Daudet told us this evening that for a very long time he had dreamed that he was a boat whose keel caused him pain; in the dream, he would turn on his side. The persistence of this dream caused him to ask [Dr] Potain if this meant his spine was rotting. Potain's response was to laugh.' (Goncourt, 9 July 1885)

Hyper-sensitivity of the skin, loss of sleep, then coughing up blood.

The 'breastplate': my first awareness of it. Suffocation, sitting up in bed, panicking.

The first moves of an illness that's sounding me out, choosing its ground.* One moment it's my eyes; floating specks; double vision; then objects appear cut in two, the page of a book, the letters of a word only half read, sliced as if by a billhook; cut by a scimitar. I grasp at letters by their downstrokes as they rush by.

My friends, the ship is sinking, I'm going down, holed below the water-line. The flag's still nailed to the mast, but there's fire everywhere, even in the water. Beginning of the end.

I don't care if my cannon-fire lands short, and the whole ship is falling apart, I'm going down fighting.

Visit to the little house, down there.†

* Daudet's son Léon (1867–1942), who trained as a doctor, noted in his memoir *Devant la Douleur* (1915) that tabes is 'fertile in atrocious surprises', and often 'likes to play with its victim', fooling him with sudden and even prolonged remissions.
† Identified (not very helpfully) by Daudet's secretary as 'the house of Monsieur X——', a morphine addict. But see p. 40.

Haven't had recourse to morphine for a long time, not since I've been taking bromide.

Spent three delightful hours there. The injection wasn't too shattering, and as always made me garrulous and took me out of myself. The day turned out all floaty, as if we'd been taking absinthe.

That evening I dined with Goncourt; hours of carefree chat until after eleven.

Bad night, woken with a jolt at three; no actual pain, but highly strung and in fear of pain. I had to take more chloral — which made three and a half grams for the night — then read for twenty minutes.

At present I'm spending time with good old Livingstone in darkest Africa. The monotony of his endless and virtually pointless journey, the constant obsession with barometric pressure and meals that rarely arrive, and the silent, calm unfolding of vast landscapes — all this makes for truly wonderful reading.

My imagination doesn't require anything more of the book than to provide a framework within which it can wander.

'Just make another three holes in my belt and tighten it a bit' — so says the trusty old madman on a day when they have nothing to eat. I would have made a fine explorer in Central Africa: I've got the sunken ribs, the eternally tightened belt, the rifts of pain, and I've lost for ever the taste for food.

Very strange, the fear that pain inspires nowadays – or rather, this pain of mine. It's bearable, and yet *I cannot bear it.* It's sheer dread: and my resort to anaesthetics is like a cry for help, the squeal of a woman before danger actually strikes.

The little house in the rue ——. I dream about it. For a long while I fight the temptation. Then I go. Immediate relief. Sweetness. The garden. A blackbird singing.

Leg cut off. No pain. Horrors.

No strength anymore. On the Boulevard Saint-Germain a carriage nearly runs me down, and I react like a berserk marionette. (Another time, in one of the walks at Champrosay, when trying to run after Zézé.)*

---

* Champrosay: village south of Paris, on the edge of the Forêt de Sénart. Daudet lived here initially in Delacroix's former atelier. In 1887 he bought a large house with grounds running down to the Seine. Goncourt's first impression was of a 'disastrously bourgeois encampment', with 'neither a painting nor an engraving nor a bibelot – not even as much as a slightly exotic straw hat'. Nevertheless, he became a constant visitor. The Daudets also had a succession of apartments in Paris.

Zézé: Daudet's younger son Lucien (1879–1946), painter, writer

Crossing the road: terrifying. Eyes don't work anymore, can't run, often can't even hurry. I have the terrors of an octogenarian. The ghoulish little old women in *Les Fleurs du mal*.*

Musing on suicide. Meeting with N——, who continues my train of thought for me, and says, 'Between the second and the third ribs.' (Strychnine.) One doesn't have the right.†

Memory. Feebleness.

------

and society figure, overshadowed by his forceful brother. A close friend of Proust, who fought a duel with a journalist for implying their relationship was homosexual. He later became companion to the aged, exiled Empress Eugénie, and indulged in 'unhappy relationships with young men of the working classes' (George Painter). Proust's housekeeper Céleste said Lucien was one of the few people Proust loved for himself, not as future material.

* 'Les Petites Vieilles' from the 'Tableaux parisiens' section; Baudelaire describes 'octogenarian Eves' who similarly move like 'marionettes' and cower before every clattering omnibus.
† 'Daudet confides in me that three or four years ago his wife, having clearly seen into his heart and read the desire to make an end of it by suicide, forestalled his confession, and made such an eloquent plea for him to live for her sake and that of the children, that he renounced his intention of killing himself.' (Goncourt, 1 December 1893)

In the Land of Pain

Ephemerality of my impressions: smoke against a wall.

Effect of intense emotions: like going down two steps at a time. You feel as if you're drawing on the very source of life itself, as if you're attacking your capital, low as it already is. I've noticed this strongly twice in the last year: once in particular, about something inane and trivial, just a stupid servants' quarrel when we were in the country. Also, during the Drumont–Meyer duel.*

And on each occasion I've felt this strange collapse of

---

* Daudet and the journalist Albert Duruy were the seconds of Edouard Drumont in his famous duel with Arthur Meyer on 24 April 1886. Drumont (1841–1917) had recently published, with Daudet's encouragement, *La France juive*, a two-volume work which did much to intensity French anti-semitism in the years before the Dreyfus case. Theodore Zeldin calls it 'not a work of observation, but a mass of falsehoods, many of them plagiarized from other works'. One such concerned Arthur Meyer (1844–1924), the founder and director of the daily *Le Gaulois*. In 1869, Carle des Perrières had published a libellously satirical portrait of Meyer, claiming that he had been thrown out of the casino at Trouville for cheating; Meyer called him out, and in the subsequent duel 'fought like a lion', according to Léon Daudet. Seventeen years later, Drumont heedlessly (or provokingly) repeated the libel; Meyer called him out too. This time Meyer, in contravention of duelling etiquette, seized his opponent's sword in his left hand while driving his own sword into Drumont's

my face and my whole body, a cutting-away, as if a knife were being wielded on my poor person.

Duruy told me how struck he'd been by this complete collapse of my features right in the middle of the drama, as we stood there on the duelling-ground. A sort of hollowing-out that doesn't go away.

What does a man's courage consist of? Nowadays, if I

———

thigh. Daudet furiously took off his coat and offered to fight Meyer on the spot.

The duel in those days often worked as a quick form of libel writ. Daudet, pugnacious by nature, had already fought two himself by this time; and even as an ataxic nearly fought two more. In 1888 he challenged the founder of *L'Evènement*, which had published an article suggesting that Mme Daudet was scheming to inherit Goncourt's estate. In 1891 he was himself challenged by the same Edouard Drumont, who had (correctly) recognized himself in *L'Obstacle*, Daudet's play on the theme of hereditary insanity. Daudet admitted fault and proposed, given his physical deterioration, that they fight at Champrosay while sitting on chairs. Eventually he signed a declaration that Drumont's father had been the sanest man that ever lived, and the matter went no further.

Drumont and Meyer were later reconciled, after Meyer declared himself anti-Dreyfusard. *La France juive* sold shamefully well: 100,000 copies in its first year, 200 editions by 1912. This pernicious tract was also republished in 1943, as the French were supplying their quota of Jews to the German death camps. The publisher of that 1943 edition was Flammarion.

take a cab and the nag starts pulling to one side, or the cabman's drunk, I get completely obsessed and terrified.

Since I became ill, I can no longer bear to see my wife* or my children lean out of a window. And if they go near the parapet of a bridge, or bend over the top of the stairs, my feet start trembling, and so do my hands. Anguish; pallor. (Remember the Pont-du-Diable, near Villemagne.)

... from the day that Pain entered my life ...

Places where I've suffered. That evening at the Z——s. The man at the piano singing, '*Gamahut, écoutez-moi donc*'.† Pallid, washed-out faces. Talking without knowing what I'm

---

* Julia Daudet, née Allard (1844–1940), also a writer, and at times her husband's collaborator. Goncourt's first impression was that she was the artist of the household rather than her husband; he also judged her the best-read woman he had ever met. 'A great artist,' he commented when she read him portions of her book *Mères et Enfants*. Jules Renard, meeting her in 1891, found her 'more artistic than me — *la femme d'art par excellence*'. Her portrait by Renoir is in the Musée d'Orsay.

† Gamahut was the assassin of Mme Ballerich, widow of a commissioner of police; he was executed in April 1885. The previous year, Aristide Bruant and Jules Joy wrote a song called '*Mad'moiselle, écoutez-moi donc*', about an old man who makes advances to a young woman, and gets his face slapped.

saying. Wandered through the reception rooms. Met Mme G——, that unfortunate woman whose sad and painful secrets are known to me. When society is their battlefield, women are capable of heroic suffering.

Every evening, a hideously painful spasm in the ribs. I read, for a long time, sitting up in bed – the only position I can endure. I'm a poor old wounded Don Quixote, sitting on his arse in his armour at the foot of a tree.

Armour is exactly what it feels like, a hoop of steel cruelly crushing my lower back. Hot coals, stabs of pain as sharp as needles. Then chloral, the *tin-tin* of my spoon in the glass, and peace at last.

This breastplate has had me in its grip for months. I can't undo the straps; I can't breathe.

At night I wander the corridors and hear four o'clock strike, from all sorts of clocks and church towers, near and far, over a period of ten minutes.

Why doesn't everyone keep the same time? Various explanations occur to me. Essentially: our lives are so different one from the other, that it makes sense for the disparity to be symbolized in this way.

The nearby barracks.* Young, loud, healthy voices.

* The *caserne Bellechasse* (Daudet was then living in the rue Bellechasse).

Windows lit up all night, like white patches at the end of a dark corridor.

How much I suffered last night, in my heel and in my ribs. Sheer torture . . . there are no words to express it, only howls of pain could do so.

Are words actually any use to describe what pain (or passion, for that matter) really feels like? Words only come when everything is over, when things have calmed down. They refer only to memory, and are either powerless or untruthful.

No general theory about pain. Each patient discovers his own, and the nature of pain varies, like a singer's voice, according to the acoustics of the hall.*

---

* Proust, in *Contre Sainte-Beuve*, describes how he could scarcely look Daudet in the eye when they met: 'I remembered to what extent bodily pain, so slight compared to his that no doubt he would have enjoyed it as a respite, had made me deaf and blind to other people, to life, to everything except my wretched body, towards which my mind was stubbornly bent, like a sick man lying in bed with his face turned to the wall.' Proust was astonished and impressed by the way 'the beautiful sick man' held forth on life and literature. At one point Daudet left the room and continued the discussion through the open doorway, while evidently giving himself a morphine injection. He returned with sweat on his brow but exuding 'the serenity of victory'.

Morphine. Its effects on me. The attacks of nausea are getting worse.

At times, my hand trembles so much that it's impossible for me to write, especially if I'm standing up.

(Signing the register at Victor Hugo's funeral. People all around, watching me — dreadful. The other day too, at the Crédit Lyonnais in the rue Vivienne.)

My brain is still holding together, but my capacity for feeling is losing its edge. I am no longer as good as I was.[*]

I walk with more confidence when I can see my own shadow, just as I walk better when someone is alongside me.

I sometimes wonder if I shouldn't apply for a course of Pasteur's inoculations: the strong analogy between my

---

[*] 'Nervous illness raises to the power of two — squares, as the algebrists put it — both the qualities and faults of those it touches. It sharpens them like pencils, as my father used to put it. The miser becomes a hyper-miser ... the jealous man surpasses Othello, the lover turns frenetic ... On the other hand, noble, generous, disinterested souls acquire, in the face of incessant pain, a strengthened sense of altruism; an almost saintly goodness blossoms forth. Such was the case with Alphonse Daudet.' (Léon Daudet, *Devant la Douleur*)

extreme bouts of pain, my furious shaking and writhing, my drowning-man contortions, and a fit of rabies.

Yes, that's right: the top of the ladder of nervous diseases, the highest rung, the apogee — is rabies.

I've been nervy and bad-tempered all day. And then Julia sight-reads a folio of gypsy music for me. Outside there's a storm, hail, thunder — inside, I relax at last.

Am briefly humiliated by thinking of myself as a mere barometer, glassed-in and marked-off. Then I console myself by realizing that the atmospheric pressure within this particular barometer governs more than just a column of mercury. Ideas flood into my brain, and I can claim to have discovered a few small laws of human behaviour — of the kind best kept to oneself.

A gentle return to work. Very happy with the state of my brain. Full of ideas, and the phrases come fairly easily, but it seems to me that coordination is now more difficult. It may just be that I'm out of the habit of writing. The factory's lain idle for the last six months; no smoke from those tall chimneys.

What we want diminishes to fill the smaller space available. Today, I don't even want to get better — just to keep on at the same level.

If they'd told me as much a year ago.

The side-effects of bromide decrease in terms of depression and memory loss. Unfortunately, its curative powers also decrease.

For some time, chloral has given me a good night's sleep; but it means I wake up tired and on edge, just as I used to in the old days when I suffered from insomnia.

Effect of chloral on the skin: thick patches like make-up.

Morphine gives you wakeful nights in which you are gently rocked in a heavenly manner.
The garden awakening. The blackbird: his song making a pattern on the pale window – a pattern drawn, warbled with the tip of his beak.

Morphine nights: the effect of chloral. Erebus,* thick

* A place of darkness between Earth and Hades.
In 1895, Daudet answered a survey of the famous by a certain Dr Lacassagne; for the previous five to six years, he said, he had slept only with the help of narcotics, as a consequence of which he had lost all capacity to dream.

black waves, and then sleeping on the edge of life, the void beneath. As delightful as slipping into a warm bath. You feel yourself being taken hold of, enfolded.

Pains in the morning; a feeling you've been bitten all over; but your mind is clear, perhaps even sharper – or simply rested.

Attempt to sleep without chloral. You close your eyes and chasms open to right and left. Five-minute cat-naps filled with harrowing nightmares: skidding and sliding, crashing down, vertigo, the abyss.

Pain is always new to the sufferer, but loses its originality for those around him. Everyone will get used to it except me.

Conversations with Charcot. For a long time I refused to talk to him: I was scared of the exchange we would have. Knowing what he'd say to me. I told him, 'I've been saving you up for last.'

A fine mind which has no disdain for a writer. His style of observation: many analogies with my own, I think.

A good tête-à-tête over lunch with Charcot. A summer's day. The Latin race affected by the sun, burnt by it.

Ah, that sun – it leaves you with a backbone like molten

sugar. Whereas the North has liquor and burns itself with that.*

* J-M Charcot (1825–93), pioneer neurologist, psychotherapist and classifier of nervous diseases. Also a brilliant teacher and clinician, famous for his ability to mime tics, spasms, rigidity, and other symptoms. Freud worked with him in 1885 and translated his lectures into German. For Léon Daudet, Charcot was a diagnostician and observer of genius, a man of vast erudition and 'implacable wisdom', whose case summaries were as concentrated as an Ingres drawing; he was also without leniency towards humanity (though full of pity for animals), found the illness more interesting than the patient, and 'observed the malfunctionings of the human machine as an astronomer observes the movement of the stars'. Edmond de Goncourt thought he had 'the physiognomy of a visionary and a charlatan' and shaved his temples to give himself 'the head of a thinker'; indeed, the whole Charcot family was a collection of 'nutcases made nutty by their association with neuropaths'. Charcot also treated Turgenev, misdiagnosing his cancer as angina.

Mary Trivas (see pp. 83–4) suggests that the note about the sun and the backbone represents Charcot's preliminary, and deliberately euphemistic, diagnosis; she calls it 'a burning and poetic aetiology'. This seems plausible: although Charcot wasn't famous for tact, he certainly returned Daudet's initial admiration. Talking to the novelist made him feel 'as if he was being placed beneath an object-glass'. He also tried to get medicine and literature to work together, by founding a 'psychophysiological society', whose members included the philosopher-critic Hippolyte Taine and the historian Ernest Renan; it met a few times, but to no great effect.

In the Land of Pain

Varieties of pain.

Sometimes, on the sole of the foot, an incision, a thin one, hair-thin. Or a penknife stabbing away beneath the big toenail. The torture of 'the boot'.* Rats gnawing at the toes with very sharp teeth.

And amid all these woes, the sense of a rocket climbing, climbing up into your skull, and then exploding there as the climax to the show.

'That's the disease for you,' says Charcot.

Intolerable pains in the heel, which only calm down when I move my leg. I spend hours, sometimes half the night, with my heel clasped in my hand.

Three months later.

I start going to the shower-baths again. A bizarre new pain when they're rubbing my legs dry. It's in the tendons of the neck: on the right-hand side when they're rubbing my left leg, and the left-hand side when they're doing my

---

* Fr. *brodequins en bois*, a form of torture which involved planks of wood being roped to the sides of the legs, and then the ropes tightened with wedges until the legs were crushed. 'The boot', a Scottish equivalent, seems to have stopped at the ankles; one version, 'the boiling boot', is probably best left to the imagination.

right leg. Nerve-racking torture, enough to make you scream.

The full syringe: dentist's waiting room.*

Sense of losing control of a leg, of it slipping away from you, like something inanimate. Sometimes an involuntary *jeté*.

Earthquake, or the heaving deck of a ship. The clichéd gesture of the legs going every which way, and the arms being flung out to grab something. The limited repertoire of such clichéd gestures.

Even the simplest and most natural of actions requires an effort of will: walking, standing up, sitting down, staying upright, taking your hat off or putting it back on. It's truly horrible. The only thing the will has no effect on is the perpetual motion of the brain. It would be so good just

* 'Tonight he told me about the interesting pages he will write . . . about going to see his father-in-law for injections. He described his terrible suffering on the way there, then the calm that descended once he arrived — just like at the dentist's when the old housekeeper ushers him into that tranquil space — and then the dreamy, hashishy state in which he returned.' (Goncourt, 20 May 1886)

to be able to stop, but no, day and night the spider goes on spinning; a few hours' respite can be gained only through doses of chloral. Macbeth murdered sleep years and years ago.

Pain finds its way everywhere, into my vision, my feelings, my sense of judgement; it's an infiltration.

Long conversation with Charcot.
It's just as I thought. I've got it for life.
The news didn't deal me the blow I would have expected.*

'Every single instant of my life.' I can date each moment of my pain as Mlle de Lespinasse could date each moment of her love.†

* Charcot was notorious for his blunt speaking to patients and their families. Mme Daudet was moved to anger by the brutal way he told her that her husband was 'incurable'. He once said to a patient: 'You're in the position of a man sitting in shit with a sabre flashing above his head: either dive in or have your head cut off.' If he was being tactful, he might announce bad news in Latin.
† Mlle de Lespinasse (1732–76), salon hostess, friend of the Encyclopédistes, remembered for her desperate, Racinian love for the unworthy M. de Guibert. The critic Sainte-Beuve called her letters to him 'one of the strangest and most memorable

Since learning that I've got it for ever – and my God, what a short 'for ever' that is going to be – I've readjusted myself and started taking these notes. I'm making them by dipping the point of a nail in my own blood and scratching on the walls of my *carcere duro*.*

All I ask is not to have to change cell, not to have to descend into an *in pace*, down there where everything's black, and thought no longer exists.

Not once, neither at the doctor's, the baths, nor the spas where the disease is treated, has it ever been given its name, its real name. I have a 'disease of the bone marrow'! Even scientific books refer euphemistically to 'the nervous system'!

Crucifixion. That's what it was like the other night. The

---

monuments to passion'. The phrase Daudet quotes is from a two-line letter, which reads: 'De tous les instants de ma vie (1774). Mon ami, je souffre, je vous aime, je vous attends.' Coincidentally, Mlle de Lespinasse also lived in the rue Bellechasse and took opium for pain (in her case, the pain of thwarted love).

* 'hard', i.e., punitive, 'imprisonment'. The term is especially associated with the incarceration of Risorgimento patriots. Daudet had perhaps read Silvio Pellico's *Le mie prigioni* – said to be the most popular Italian book of the nineteenth century – about his fifteen years of *carcere duro* under the Austrians.

torment of the Cross: violent wrenching of the hands, feet, knees; nerves stretched and pulled to breaking-point. The coarse rope bound tight round the torso, the spear prodding at the ribs. The skin peeling from my hot, parched, fever-crusted lips; to slake my thirst I took a spoonful of iodized bromide, salty and bitter. It was the sponge soaked in vinegar and gall.*

I then imagined a conversation about Pain between Christ and the two thieves.

Several days of peace. Thanks no doubt to bromide and this fine hot late-June weather.

Painful hours spent at Julia's bedside . . . Fury at finding myself such a wreck, and too weak to nurse her. But my ability to feel sympathy and tenderness for others is still well alive, as is my capacity for emotional suffering, for emotional torment . . . And I'm glad of that, despite the terrible pains that returned today.†

Analysis of chloral-induced sleep. – It's over, it's a peak I shall never be able to climb again.

---

* In 1893 Eugène Carrière did a portrait of Daudet. Goncourt (31 December) described it as 'Daudet on the Cross, Daudet at Golgotha'.
† Mme Daudet fell ill in late 1890, and believed she was dying. In the event, she survived another half-century.

Thus I can count on twenty wonderful minutes between my two doses of chloral. Careful to choose what I read then: nothing but the best.* My mind is unusually lucid.

Two days of great suffering.

Spasms in the right foot, with pains shooting all the way up my sides. I feel like a one-man band, tugging on all his strings and playing all his instruments at once. 'Going to Draveil, off down the street / With strings on his elbows and strings on his feet.'† This is me: the one-man band of pain.

Pain has a life of its own. The ingenious efforts a disease makes in order to survive. People say, 'Let nature take its course.' But death is as much a part of nature as life. The forces of survival and destruction are at war within us and are equally matched. I've seen impressive examples of the skill with which disease manages to propagate itself. The two TB cases who fell in love: how passionately they clung to one another. You could almost hear the disease saying to itself, 'Now here's a perfect match!' And just imagine the morbidity it would give birth to.

* Daudet's nocturnal reading in 1890 was 'Montaigne, Rabelais, Pascal, Shakespeare and Goethe'. (Goncourt, 14 November)
† Daudet's jingle goes: '*Sur la route de Draveil, ficelles aux coudes, aux pieds . . .*' Draveil is a couple of kilometres north of Champrosay.

The way nurses talk: 'That's a lovely wound ... Now this wound is really wonderful.' You'd think they were talking about a flower.

Last night, in my study, around ten o'clock, I had a couple of minutes of pure anguish.

I was fairly calm, writing an unimportant letter. The page was very white, with all the light from a *lampe anglaise** concentrated upon it; the table and the study were plunged in darkness.

A servant came in and put a book or something on the table. I raised my head, and from that moment I lost all sense of everything for two or three minutes. I must have looked completely stupid, because the servant, taking my blank face as a question, explained what he'd come for. I didn't understand his words and no longer remember them.

What was horrible was that I didn't recognize my own study: I knew that's where I was, but had lost all sense of it as a place. I had to get up and find my bearings, running my hand along the bookcase and the doors and saying to myself, 'That's where he came in.' Gradually, my brain began to work again, my faculties returned. But I remember my

* 'English lamp': a version of the miner's lamp, adapted for domestic use.

vivid sense of the whiteness of the letter I was writing, the way it shone forth from the blackness of the table.

A kind of hypnotic effect, compounded by fatigue.

This morning, hurrying to write all this down, I remembered being in a cab a couple of years ago: I shut my eyes for a few moments, and when I opened them I found myself on the lamplit *quais* of a Paris I simply couldn't identify. I ended up leaning right out of the cab door, staring at the river and a row of grey houses opposite. I was bathed in a sweat of fear. Then, as we came to a bridge, I suddenly recognized the Palais de Justice and the Quai des Orfèvres, and the bad dream faded away.

Neuropathy. I find it impossible to write an address on an envelope when I know that people will read and examine it; whereas in the intimacy of a notebook I can guide my pen as I choose.

The change in my handwriting . . .

Tonight, pain in the form of an impish little bird hopping hither and thither, pursued by the stab of my needle; over all my limbs, then right in my joints. But the injection misses its target, then misses again, and the pain is sharper every time.

In the Land of Pain

Two or three occasions when morphine's effectiveness has been inhibited by antipyrine. Flashes of pain in the foot, muscles crushed by a waggon, spear-thrusts in the little finger.

Epigraph: *dictante dolore.**

My poor carcass is hollowed out, voided by anaemia. Pain echoes through it as a voice echoes in a house without furniture or curtains. There are days, long days, when the only part of me that's alive is my pain.

After taking a great deal of acetanilide — which turns the lips blue and annihilates the already battered self — I've just completed a year on antipyrine. Two or three grams per day. Every eight to ten days, small doses of morphine. Antipyrine is a joyless drug, and for some while has had cruel consequences for the stomach and intestines.[†]

* 'with pain dictating', 'pain dictates the words I now write'. Ovid has *'dolor dictat'*; Silius Italicus has *'dolor verba aspera dictat'*.
[†] acetanilide: used as an analgesic and antipyretic (fever preventative). Daudet, his lips blue from the drug, confided to Goncourt its more unwelcome side-effects: 'My arse-hole, instead of wanting to expel things, seems to want to suck them up. It's like an octopus. When I have an enema, I'm afraid it's going to swallow up the pump. And I'm not even producing little goat-turds any more, just bird-shit, plus from time to time a very small liquorice stick.' (Goncourt, 6 October 1887)

Suspension. Seyre's apparatus.

The hanging up of poor ataxics, which takes place at Keller's in the evening, is a grim business. The Russian they hang up in a seated position. Two brothers; the little dark one writhing away.

I am suspended in the air for four minutes, the last two solely by my jaw. Pain in the teeth. Then, as they let me down and unharness me, a terrible pain in my back and the nape of my neck, as if all the marrow was melting: it forces me to crouch down on all fours and then very slowly stand up again while – as it seems to me – the stretched marrow finds its rightful place again.

No observable benefit.*

Thirteen suspensions. Then I start coughing blood.

* The Seyre suspension was a new treatment for ataxia, imported from Russia by Charcot: it was intended to stretch the spine and loosen the joints. Daudet told Goncourt that the suspensions took place in a dark corner of the baths, after everyone had left, under the supervision of the hydrotherapist Dr Keller. His description of these crepuscular hangings made Goncourt think of Goya. As for their effectiveness: later that same year (1889) Goncourt records the case of an ataxic who recovered the use of both his arms and legs after his second suspension, and his 'mad joy' at once again being able to hand a news vendor three sous for *Le Figaro*. He seems to have been the exception.

I attribute this to a congestion of the lungs brought on by the fatiguing effects of the treatment.

It's all going ... Darkness is gathering me into its arms.

Farewell wife, children, family, the things of my heart ...

Farewell me, cherished me, now so hazy, so indistinct ...

In bed. Dysentery. Two injections of morphine a day, about twenty degrees. No longer able to get out of the habit. My stomach has adapted itself a little: with five or six drops, I no longer vomit, although I can't eat. Forced to continue taking chloral.

If I've taken morphine beforehand, I sleep very well. But if I have an injection during the night, after the chloral, then my sleep is interrupted and there's no chance of any more for the rest of the night. Restlessness, all my thoughts in turmoil, a frenetic succession of images, projects, themes — a magic lantern. The next day, my head is filled with smoke, I get the shivers.

Each injection stops the pain for three or four hours. Then come 'the wasps', the stinging and stabbing here, there and everywhere — followed by the Pain, that cruel guest.

Astonishment and joy at finding others who suffer as

you do. Duchesne de Boulogne coming to wake up old Privat one evening: 'They're ataxic, the lot of them!'*

X——'s life story now strikes me as all the more heart-breaking. A life in the shadows, tormented by the 'disease of the marrow' he dragged around with him, and that no one understood at the time. 'Oh, that X——,' they used to say, 'he's just a hypochondriac.' Laughed at by those close to him for his enemas, his infusions of marsh mallow, and so on.

* Duchesne (*or* Duchenne) de Boulogne, neurologist (1806–75), who pioneered the use of electricity in medicine, and was the first to make the connection between syphilis and locomotor ataxia. He was invited to Lamalou (see p. 59) by Dr Privat, who had established the modern spa both medically and commercially. Léon Daudet reported Duchenne de Boulogne arriving at Lamalou one evening, looking out of his window the next morning, and seeing such an array of classic symptoms parading beneath him that he rushed into his host's bedroom, waking him up, shouting, 'They're all ataxic. They belong to me. I'm going to question all of them, all of them.'

In *La Doulou* Daudet uses *ataxie* and *ataxique* (the latter as both adjective and noun) rather than the higher-medical *tabès* and *tabétique*; I have followed his usage. Tabes denotes the disease process in the nervous system, and ataxia its most visible outward consequence; Daudet allows the latter to include the former.

S—— claims that bromide calms him down, makes him sensible, dogmatic, turns him into Prudhomme.*

The way his father lives, never sitting down to eat, always on the move, pecking away at various plates laid out all around the dining room.

I was meeting X and his patient at the station. All the symptoms. The way this plutocrat now looks. He's had handles installed in his house, and a sort of handrail or banister to cling to when he has an attack. Sleeps standing up, like a horse at its manger.

I had him very much in mind when I wrote L'Evangéliste. I set the image of a man like him against the backdrop of the railway, the train arriving, the express, with the house of D—— R—— visible.†

---

* Joseph Prudhomme, a character invented by the writer and caricaturist Henri Monnier (1805–77) to typify self-satisfied mediocrity and sonorous banality.

† L'Evangéliste (1883), a novel leisurely in manner but fierce in theme, about the harmful effects of evangelical religion backed by big money. The (Protestant) evangelist of the title is Mme Autheman, who in the service of God deforms every life she touches. Her husband, a Jewish banker who has converted, suffers from a large, disfiguring birthmark on his cheek which he keeps covered with a black cloth: Daudet refers to it as a 'dreadful hereditary naevus'. Worse, the banker finds himself supplanted in his wife's heart by

X—— tells me about his father-in-law. The daughter has been nursing him day and night for eight years; washing him, turning him over, cutting his toenails and fingernails. She's given over her life to that. Then he dies with no more than a squeak. The open-mouthed stupefaction of the poor woman in the face of such littleness, this nothing of a life which has been snuffed out all the same. 'Isn't she going to remember to shut her mouth,' thought X—— irritatedly. A final washing of the body, and that was it. Now she's quite alone, and doesn't know what to do, whom to love, whom to nurse. She's like a prisoner released from Melun after a long incarceration, suddenly finding herself outside in the street.

Read Xavier Aubryet's 'La Maladie à Paris'. Ill for four years. His agonies in the street. Generosity of Brébant; charity of the Maison d'Or.

Morphine injections. Amputee.

Very Catholic: 'This is all I have . . . At least leave me my God!'

―――

the Lord. Deprived of both love and sex, lacking the temperament to console himself with prostitutes, Autheman decides to kill himself. Earlier he has dreamed of sleeping with his disfigurement pressed against the cold metal of the railway line; now he throws himself beneath the evening express within sight of his wife's large country HQ. Daudet dedicated the novel to Charcot.

Cared for at the end by a *vivandière* who terrified him. Claudin's viciousness.

Hands all curled up, but still some use. Blind at the end. Groping his way towards death. Intense pains.

Xavier Aubryet getting indignant because people couldn't be bothered with him. (For myself, I'd like to be left alone in the country for a year, seeing no one but my wife. The children could come once a week.)

At least La Madeleine didn't show himself.

He ended up in the Midi, near Carpentras; at his sister's place in the country.

One day he thinks about the Café Riche, about sitting there with a rug over his knees, gazing in despair at the boulevard which killed him, and which killed Aubryet.

The table at the Café Riche opposite that of the Café Anglais. Mental torture.*

---

* Xavier Aubryet (1827–80), journalist, editor, literary man-about-town, whose loquacity and taste for paradox enchanted some and infuriated others. 'If you lived with him,' wrote Goncourt, 'you'd have to buy a revolver and tell him you'd blow his brains out unless he agreed to say only simple things.' Aubryet's syphilis eventually left him paralysed, blind, and lacking any sense of taste; though like Daudet he retained his intellectual faculties to the end. 'La Maladie à Paris' is an acerbic essay on the 'social death' that sickness

A day at Auteuil. In a garden full of roses, with gentle sunshine and the smell of warm blossom, I can't escape the image of poor Jules, sitting there in a stupor, a straw hat on his head, 'away in space, in empty space'.*

———

provokes. 'Illness and Paris are mutually exclusive terms; Paris only likes healthy people, because it only likes success, and illness is as much a failure as poverty.'

Brébant and La Maison d'Or were both restaurants (the famous Magny dinners transferred to Brébant in 1869). Gustave Claudin (1823–96) was a *Figaro* journalist, and Henri de la Madèlene [*sic*] (1825–87) a novelist and columnist. The Café Riche (16, boulevard des Italiens) and the Café Anglais (corner of boulevard des Italiens and the rue Marivaux) were frequented by journalists and literary men. For the consequences of patronizing the Café Anglais, see p. 71.

* Edmond de Goncourt and his brother Jules were so inseparable that in twenty-two years after the death of their mother they were only twice apart for as much as twenty-four hours; so inseparable that they wrote their joint diary in the first person. They moved to Auteuil in 1868; Jules died from tertiary syphilis in 1870. During his final decline, Edmond asked him, 'Where are you, my dear chap?' and after a few moments Jules replied, 'Away in space, in empty space.' After Jules' death, Daudet became Edmond's closest friend, literary confidant and surrogate brother — whereupon Edmond had to witness a harrowing syphilitic decline for the second time. Daudet, for his part, used to quiz Goncourt about Jules' symptoms, comparing them with his own.

In the Land of Pain

Jules de Goncourt and Baudelaire. Writers' illnesses. Aphasia.

For a month I've been taken up with the idea of the end of the world. I've had an exact vision of how it would be. Then I read that Baudelaire, during the final lucid period of his life, was also obsessed by the same literary idea. Aphasia arrived shortly afterwards . . .*

Add Leopardi to the list of my forebears, my doppel-gangers in pain.

The great Flaubert, what a struggle it was for him to find the right words. Surely it must have been the enormous quantity of bromide he ingested that made the dictionary rebel against him?

I suggested a thesis topic to my son: Pascal's neurosis.†

---

* The title 'La Fin du monde' appears in various lists of Baudelaire's projected prose poems and in a list of 'Romans et nouvelles'. It seems to have been a recurrent literary idea, rather than the terminal notion Daudet supposes.

† 'Pascal was a neurotic in the full meaning of the word . . . He spent his life dying.' (Daudet in conversation with *La Chronique médicale*, 15 February 1896). On the flyleaf of his copy of *Les Pensées*, Daudet listed Pascal's symptoms: 'hydrophobia', 'paralysis of the

One evening, about eleven, when the house was asleep and the lights were out, a knock at the door. 'It's me.' X—— comes in for a minute, sits down and stays two hours. Fascinating confession about the suicidal impulse which possesses him. His elder brother, his grandfather, etc. His account of O. X——. Hatred for his brother. O——'s nervous disease: in the head; the legs attacked as well. I know that kind of mechanical, boxed-in stiffness.

Heinrich Heine is much on my mind. I feel his illness was similar to mine.

I wonder if I shouldn't add Jean-Jacques to my list of ancestral doppelgangers in pain. Wasn't his bladder disease, as it often may be, a warning sign and side-effect of 'disease of the marrow'?*

---

legs', ending with 'locomotor ataxia' – an attempt to enlist him as a fellow-sufferer *avant la lettre* (see p. 82). Léon Daudet, who studied under Charcot, had a dream in 1889 in which the neurologist was carrying Pascal's skull and a copy of *Les Pensées*. The skull was segmented like a dried-up honeycomb, and Charcot was demonstrating exactly which *pensée* originated from which cell.

* Daudet's literary 'doppelgangers in pain'. Leopardi suffered constantly (spine, lungs, stomach, eyes), though not venereally: he

Morphine.

The irreplaceable anaesthetic.

The imbecilic rages it stirs up.*

But wasn't opium doing the same job previously? Benjamin Constant and Mme de Staël used it to excess. I see from Heinrich Heine's correspondence that he took a strong dose every day. It's strange to follow the poet's illness through the three volumes of his business letters; it starts with neuralgia when he was 'just a lad', and ends with him confined to his bed for eight years, in torment.

almost certainly never had sex in his life. Voltaire started the rumour that Rousseau suffered from venereal disease (Rousseau himself said he merely had a 'malformation' with fluctuating effects); the 'bladder disease' was supposedly stones blocking the urethra. Flaubert contracted syphilis in Egypt, though the disease did not progress. Heine's case was indeed the closest to Daudet's: bedridden with tabes, he complained of his 'mattress-grave'. The landscape painter Félix Zem shook Daudet's hand in 1886, and was reminded of the hand Heine had extended from his bed: 'the heat, not of a fever, but of a quite different kind'.

* 'Daudet hasn't done any work for about ten days. I asked him if morphine prevented him from working, and he replied, "Yes, with morphine you never get beyond general ideas."' (Goncourt, 3 August 1889). 'I'm trying to reduce my intake of morphine to one injection a day. It makes me jumpy, irritable and spiteful, yes spiteful to my wife and children.' (Goncourt, 10 October 1889)

If I were to write in praise of morphine, I'd talk about the little house in the rue——. Well, that's all over now. My old companion, who used to give me injections, is dead.*

Deep emotion when they brought his watch to my bedside; also his Pravaz syringe, his sharpening stone, and his needles, which all of a sudden seemed to come alive, turn into a swarm of poisonous leeches, living biting things – rattlesnakes, asps – Cleopatra's basket of figs.

It would be a good thing to write about, that shuttered life of his, a life without serious pain, almost all of it spent in bed these past few years. Books, journals, newspapers, a little painting. And the watch, in its box, regulating this static, attenuated existence.

He clung on to it, this life that he had. Just one fear: that his final passage would be a torment.

My poor friend. It's all over now.

The clever way death cuts us down, but makes it look like just a thinning-out. Generations never fall with one blow – that would be too sad and too obvious. Death prefers to do it piecemeal. The meadow is attacked from several sides at the same time. One of us goes one day; another some time afterwards; you have to stand back and look

* His father-in-law, Jules Allard (died 9 March 1889).

around you to take in what's missing, to grasp the vast slaughter of your generation.

You have to die so many times before you die . . .

Two and a half years without making notes.
I've worked. I've suffered.
Disheartenment. Exhaustion.
The same old song, again and again; the shower-baths; Lamalou.

For the last year, problems with my legs. Can't go down a staircase if there isn't a handrail; can't walk across a waxed floor. Sometimes I feel as if I don't own part of myself — the lower half. *My legs get confused.*

A change in my condition: walking badly. Not being able to walk at all.

For a long time I had a horror of the invalid carriage; I would hear it coming, trundling towards me. Nowadays I think about it less, and no longer with the same dread. Apparently you suffer much less by the time you get to that stage . . . Not to be in pain anymore . . .

Morphine injection. Several times in a certain part of my leg. Result: a stinging followed by an unbearable burning feeling in the back, the upper torso, the face and the hands. A subcutaneous feeling, doubtless insignificant but still terrifying: you feel you're heading for an apoplectic fit.

The above written during one of these crises.

The imbeciles who imagine that I've come to Venice solely in order to be received by the Emperor of Germany for a few minutes.*

As if Pain were not already the most despotic and possessive of Imperial hostesses!

I'd like to be earthed in like a mole, and live alone, all alone.

Pain, you must be everything for me. Let me find in you all those foreign lands you will not let me visit. Be my philosophy, be my science.

My old friend Montaigne: he had a special pity for physical suffering.†

---

* Newspapers had speculated that William II, on an official visit to Venice in April 1896, would receive the writer.
† Mme Daudet complained that whenever Daudet read Montaigne, he ceased to be the Daudet she knew; ceased to be the loving husband and father, and became 'shrivelled up, hard-hearted'. For Mme Daudet, Montaigne's philosophy was egotistical, pessimistic and base, while his attitude to women was 'abominable'.

In the Land of Pain

Pain leads to moral and intellectual growth. But only up to a certain point.

A wounded Don Juan; Don Juan as amputee. That would make a good play. To show the man who has 'known them all' as jealous of other men, sapped by illness, a peg-legged eavesdropper, bleeding, cowardly, raging, tearful.

I feel like some creature from mythology, whose torso is locked in a box of wood or stone, gradually turning numb and then solid. As the paralysis spreads upwards, the sick man changes into a tree or a rock, like some nymph from Ovid's *Metamorphoses*.

Nothing more dreadful than all this struggling.
At least the day will come when you can't move any more . . .

Effect of morphine.
Wake up in the night, with nothing beyond a mere sense of existing. But the place, the time, and any personal sense of self, are completely lost.
Not a single idea.
Sense of EXTRAORDINARY moral blindness.

Unable to control my movements in the night.

Part one: locked in.

Wanted a prison so that I could shout: that's where I am.

Can't move!

And next?

What's terrible is the gradual increase in sorrow, in punishment.

He names me as executor of his will. This is an affectionate and thoughtful gesture: he wants to make me believe I'll live longer than him.*

The prisoner imagines freedom to be more wonderful than it is.

The patient imagines good health to be a source of ineffable pleasure — which it isn't.

All that we lack is a sense of the divine.

Can't get down my front steps at Champrosay unaided; nor at Goncourt's house. O Pascal!†

---

* 'He' is Edmond de Goncourt, who made Daudet his executor in 1887. Goncourt's gesture was justified: Daudet outlived him by eighteen months.

† Perhaps a reference to Pascal's famous example of needless vertigo as evidence of the power of the imagination: 'Place the greatest philosopher in the world on a plank which is well broad enough,

In the Land of Pain

Pain in the country: a veil over the horizon. Those roads, with their pretty little bends — all they provoke in me now is the desire to flee. To run away, to escape my sickness.

Not being able to give alms any more is one of my hardships. The pleasure it used to give me. The beggar with his eager hand, and suddenly a hundred sous land in it.*

Sterility. That's the only word that gets close to describing the horrible stagnation into which the mind can fall. It's the condition believers call accidie. — This note, made quickly, is wooden, inexpressive, solipsistic; but it was written during cruel illness.

For half the night handwritings of all kinds, and from all periods of my life — from the scripts of school friends to my father's hieroglyphs and his 'Louis XIV commercial' style — pass before my eyes, then turn and spin as if in a

---

but with a precipice beneath him. His reason may convince him he is safe, but his imagination will prevail. Few will not turn pale and sweat at the mere thought of it.'

* Commenting on Daudet's earlier note about being 'not as good as I was', André Ebner insisted that he was 'a veritable minister of charity' in the final twelve years of his life.

gyroscope. By the morning I was completely shattered . . . The end is near.

In the morning my hands are obstinately curled up on top of the sheet, like dead leaves, deprived of sap.*

Vision of Christ on the Cross, in the morning, on Golgotha. Mankind. Screams.

This morning all my feelings have lost their edge, like after a night of over-indulgence. The effect of using the same anaesthetics for too long.

I don't want my next book to be too harsh. Last time I felt I went too far. Poor humanity – you shouldn't tell it everything. I shouldn't inflict on people what I've endured, this painful, all too self-aware end to my life. People should be treated as if they were sick; it's a question of striking the right balance, of proper consideration; let's make them love the doctor, rather than play the tough and brutal butcher.

* 'The comparison Daudet uses when describing how his hands look in the morning: the constant spasms make them curl up like *dry leaves*. This comparison lodges in my brain for the entire day.' (Goncourt, 31 May 1886)

And I would deserve credit for this next book,* which would be tender, virtuous and indulgent, because I am in great pain. Pride in not imposing on others the bad moods and the sombre injustices of my suffering.

From time to time, a memory of the active life, of happier times. For instance, those Neapolitan coral-fishermen among the rocks, in the evening. The epitome of physical well-being.

Return to childhood. To reach that distant chair, to cross that waxed corridor, requires as much effort and ingenuity as Stanley deploys in the African jungle.[†]

My anguish is great, and I weep as I write.

---

* *La Petite Paroisse* (1895), his penultimate novel. The book in which he 'went too far' was *L'Immortel* (1888), his novel about the Académie française.

† Daudet called H. M. Stanley 'the tourist version of Napoleon'. This was the highest praise: the two figures he admired most in his century were Bonaparte and 'Hamlet', as he referred to George Meredith. On a visit to London with his son Léon, Daudet met both Stanley and Meredith. Later, his enthusiasm for the literature of exploration (see p. 8) shifted to the polar zones. In bed, he would read to Mme Daudet about the Arctic, and she would fall asleep.

To think that one day you could become a burden like this, that you could put your family to flight . . .

Dread. Anguish in my heart. Since I've been left alone with pain, the life I have known has been so harsh.

We also inflict wounds, wounds to the pride of those who love us.

The power of actually being there: I have learnt it to my cost, since I became someone unable to walk, someone no longer visible.

The transfer from *carcere duro* to *durissimo*.
Nothing but terror and despair at first; then, gradually, the mind, like the body, adjusts to this appalling condition.
See the dialogues of Leopardi, Tasso in prison, etc.

My existence is effectively over: I live only through the novel – that's to say, through the lives of others.*

* Further: 'We talked about living on after death through one's work, a preoccupation for my brother and me, and still one for me. Daudet said that he views survival entirely in terms of his children; a book was simply the result of an act of expansiveness, an expenditure of energy, which could equally have manifested itself differently.' (Goncourt, 25 September 1887)

In the Land of Pain

Life consists of antagonism.

Struggle against those of ill will, shifting reefs which hole the ship below the waterline.

I only know one thing, and that is to shout to my children, 'Long live Life!' But it's so hard to do, while I am ripped apart by pain.

II

In the Land of Pain

This year at Néris* either my eyes are less sharp or the company is less interesting. A few characters, however. Mme M——, magistrate's wife, organizer of parties and outings, a fat matron living it up with a bunch of junior prosecutors. 'Let's have some champagne and be jolly! You're not *jolly!*' The receptions at Châteaudun . . . Two daughters, one tall and horse-faced, with pretensions to elegance and a pile of dresses in her trunk; the younger one, twelve, a strange child with dark expressionless eyes and clownish movements, who has fainting-fits and is brought out of them by the mother passing in front of her eyes her golden 'lucky charm'. The physical stance of a monkey and a sleepwalker. What the wife tells us about her husband — his quirks and fads, his hypochondria and addiction to every kind of illness. The unnecessary operation on his eyes. When he takes the waters with his wife and children, he always

* A thermal station in the Allier; Daudet was sent there by his friend Dr Potain in 1882, and returned in 1884. Potain had previously sent him to take the waters at Allevard in the Isère.

stays at a different hotel. On their honeymoon, the bedroom divided into two: 'This is your side . . . This is mine . . . Those are your chairs . . . These are mine.' And he's a judge, this headcase! Memory of a picnic lunch – the wife lying flat on her back, feet higher than her head, with her false plait removed and lying coiled beside her like a grass snake.

The Women On Their Own. Mme T——. 'As clever as a man' (?), 'a pupil of D——', Jewish head, long, glistening, grooved eyes, Parisian chatter, an affair with the Casino cellist who was discovered doing up his cravat in the little sitting room at five in the morning. Mme L——, a short woman with an affected smile, the corners of her mouth always turned up, faded, mysterious, timid, lacking social graces, arriving at the dinner table with twigs and bunches of flowers threaded through her belt, then becoming ashamed and embarrassed, and shiftily ripping away this ceremonial garland.

The other type of Woman On Her Own. Nice Mme S—— and her friend Mlle de X——. Both have the look of *soeurs tourières*,* and scoot off to church as soon as the meal

---

* Convent entrances contained a *tour*, or 'turn', a cylindrical box on pivots through which small objects could be passed in and out of the building. The *soeurs tourières* who presided over this device were allowed contact with the outside world, and were presumably chosen for their affable nature.

is over. Mlle de X—— is gushy, plump, kind-hearted, naïve, full of convent gossip, proud of her two sisters who married money, and of her family, penniless minor Breton nobility who breed as fast as a fishing village when the boats come in. Taken up by Mme S——. She displays widowhood, virtue, religion, has kindly eyes, and is a bit cracked. Her husband was killed by her father in a hunting accident; deep into charitable works; no children.

Mme C——, still young, widow of a naval officer, ugly, eyes too black, red blotches on her nose, which she constantly examines with the aid of a little hand-mirror. Wherever she looks she sees scorpions, spiders, bloodstained hands. She's always alone, walking through the orchard with tiny steps, then sitting motionless on a bench for hours, hand on cheek, sunk in thought. She makes the hotel feel like a madhouse.

And then there's Mme P——, the General's wife. They call her 'Mother of the Constabulary'. She's been coming to the hotel for ten years, which gives her an authority she guards jealously. A desire to please, and also to conquer. All the guests, on both arrival and departure, go and present their respects! She's an old flirt, a self-invented character, a 'Milady' still chomping away hard with her dentures.

This resort for anaemics has its funny side. No one remembers anyone's name; brains are racked all the time;

there are great holes in the conversation. It took ten of us to come up with the word 'industrial'.

Never before have my poor old nerves been rubbed so raw by the promiscuous contact of hotel life. I loathed watching my neighbours eat: the toothless mouths and diseased gums; the toothpicks jabbing away at crevices in the molars; the diners who can only eat on one side, the tireless masticators, noisy gnawers, brutal carnivores. Bestial humanity! All those jaws working away, those greedy eyes fixed frantically on the plate, those furious glances when a dish doesn't arrive on time. I watched all this and found it nauseating; it quite put me off my food.

Not to mention all the digestive turmoil: the two WCs at the end of the corridor, side by side and lit by the same gas-lamp, so that you heard every constipatory groan, every burst of colonic plentitude, every rustle of paper. The horror . . . the horror of life!

And all the gossip going round the hotel about the guests' infirmities, their bizarre habits, their absurd little illnesses . . .

At Néris I spotted the professor of mathematics from Clermont. The first person I've seen with the same problem as me, but a more advanced case.

I see him in my mind's eye, putting one foot down carefully in front of the other, but still tottery: as if walking on ice. Sad. The hotel maids said that he pissed his bed.

The resort for neuropaths. Figures on crutches glimpsed on country lanes, suddenly appearing in the gaps between high hedges; weird and unexpected tales of woe; poor simple country women worn away by pain. — Mud-baths in a forest in the North. A strange set-up. A sort of glassed-in rotunda built over a swamp of black mud which they shove you down into forcibly. The delightful feeling as this warm wet glue soaks into your whole body. Some go in right up to their necks, others only as far as their arms. There are about sixty of us, all piled in higgledy-piggledy, laughing, chatting away, or just reading with the help of wooden floats. There aren't any bugs in the mud, but thousands of little warm water-spurts which tickle you gently.

The provincial family I met at Néris. The husband, old and bent, with pendulous grey moustaches and a few flat, dangling locks of hair; his sad face, with its sardonic smile but kindly eye, was topped off by a Raphael-style velveteen cap. This was P——, flower-painter, pupil of Saint-Jean.* The wife, tall, thin, flat-chested and pretentious, wearing her hat Rembrandt-style, runs a nursing-home for ladies. She's

---

*Simon Saint-Jean (1808–60) was a highly regarded flower-painter, chosen to represent Lyonnais flower design at the Great Exhibition of 1851.

spoiled and pampered, but you get the sense that she puts the bread on the table while he pursues artistic glory. Accompanying them is a fat, deaf, whiskery girl, one of Madame's boarders, who follows them around like a lady's maid and prepares café-cognacs in their room to save money. 'Monsieur P——,' she calls from the window, and her flutey voice contains a touch of coquettish mystery, as if she were announcing that it was time for his colonic irrigation.

LAMALOU

L amalou.* The Ataxia Polka. The establishment. In the Middle Ages, shirts impregnated with sulphur. The baths; windows; shameful traces. Music. Plays. Tall mantelpieces; wood fires; roughcast walls.

* A thermal station north of Béziers, in the spurs joining the Cévennes to the Montagne Noire. The waters, known since Roman times, were advised for rheumatic and nervous illnesses, especially tabes. There were three springs: at Lamalou-le-Haut (the hottest), Lamalou-le-Centre and Lamalou-le-Bas (the most popular). Daudet first went there in 1885, and returned annually until 1893; he stayed at the Hôtel Mas, directly opposite the Casino and the Theatre. (All three buildings are still there, the hotel due to reopen after refurbishment.) Other visitors to Lamalou included Alexandre Dumas *fils*, Sully-Prudhomme (first winner of the Nobel Prize for Literature) and Gide. Léon Daudet wrote that there were 'few places as beautiful, as sombre, as grim and as touching' as Lamalou.

Charcot made the spa's fortune by sending many of his patients there. Alphonse Daudet complained in 1891: 'Can you believe that a man like Charcot hasn't once been to Lamalou, hasn't once gone to study the effect of what he prescribes on the beings for whom he prescribes it? Doctors are very poor at discovering things. When a patient says to them, "I've noticed that an egg taken in the

In the hotel courtyard, the to-and-fro of patients. A march-past of different diseases, each more dreadful than the previous one. Analogy between all illnesses; eyes either feverish or lifeless. Blue sky, glittering light — lemon trees growing in large Anduze pots.

Patients giving one another advice:
'This is what you have to do.'
'But does it work?'
'No.'
'Are you any better?'
'No.'

---

morning on an empty stomach brought me relief on such-and-such a day", they note the observation and issue the same prescription to all their patients.' Charcot may not have visited Lamalou, but the town knew how to salute a benefactor, erecting the Fontaine Charcot in 1903, ten years after the neurologist's death. Léon Daudet thought that Duchenne de Boulogne deserved a statue more than Charcot did. In the event, the Fontaine Charcot is at the end of the avenue Charcot, off which runs the rue Duchenne de Boulogne, which intersects with the rue Daudet, whose continuation is the rue Privat, in which a bust of Dr Privat is to be found. According to Léon Daudet, Charcot preferred his English and Russian patients to his German ones, whom he found 'annoying'. In 1944 the Germans annoyingly removed his bronze bust from the top of the Fountain; it was eventually replaced by a stone replica in 1955.

'So why are you giving me advice?'
Lunacy.

Women, Sisters of Charity, nurses, Antigones.
Russians, inscrutable Asiatics.
Priests.
Music: like a morphine injection.
Rages.
The Ambitious One, the 'Napoleon Who Never Made It', in the bath.
The crazies.
The chatterboxes.
They're like this not just because they're from the Midi, but because of nervous illness.

My doppelganger. The fellow whose illness most closely resembles your own. How you love him, and how you make him tell you everything! I've got two such, an Italian painter and a member of the Court of Appeal. Between them, these two comprise my suffering.*

* And also its future: 'Poor Daudet, who is haunted by an *idée fixe*: the fear of degradation, and the physical shame which paralysis entails. And when you try to reassure him, he tells you that he has studied the progression of his disease among his fellow-sufferers at Lamalou: he knows what will happen to him next year, and what will happen to him the year after.' (Goncourt, 14 July 1890)

The Theatre at Lamalou.
Entry of the ataxics. Sleep of the dead.

The conductor and first violin of the Theatre band, married to the duenna, plays and conducts with his baby asleep across his knees. Delightful.

It's hilarious, this land of neurotics, filled with shouting, trumpet-calls, sirens. 'Upper Pain' – mountain accents, one street, hay-wains, carriages travelling ostentatiously at walking pace, the panicking ataxics, bicycles, muleteers. 'Upper Pain' and 'Lower Pain' are at daggers drawn.*

A. B——, an impressive chatterbox, hectic and passionate, the opposite of aphasic; eats by himself to save energy.

---

* Daudet is punning on Lamalou-le-Haut/Bas and La Doulou-le-Haut/Bas. At a dinner for the Daudets' silver wedding in 1892, Goncourt found himself placed next to Mme Munkaczy, the flamboyant and tactless wife of a Hungarian painter. Edmée (1886–1937), the Daudets' third child and only daughter (and Goncourt's godchild), had been conceived at Lamalou. Mme Munkaczy said to Daudet, 'It's too funny, this child of Lamalou ... They say the place normally has the opposite effect, don't they?' Glancing over to her husband, who was at a neighbouring table, she went on, 'Well, obviously you went to Upper Lamalou and he went to Lower Lamalou.'

IN THE LAND OF PAIN

Dr B——, listening to Brachet, commented, 'Hmm, that's very useful.'

You can say that again!*

In the dining room: the man who quite suddenly finds himself unable to read the menu. His wife bursts into tears and leaves the table . . .

Lamalou. The little Spanish girl, somewhere between twelve and sixteen, with flat, pomaded hair. Red dress, pendulous earrings, long yellowish face resting on a skeletal hand; at night she sleeps in a sitting position. Fear of rats; so she's not given a room on the ground floor.

The Spaniard who was taken ill on his boat and has lost the use of his legs; a gangling Robinson Crusoe silhouette; carried around by his servant; espadrilles, white cap; the darling of the hotel maids.

The fellow from the Haute-Marne, asleep in the sun, infested with flies. He eats out of doors, and morphine always makes him vomit — rain or shine, indoors or outdoors. 'What's the point?' he asks.

---

* Daudet considered Auguste Brachet (1844–98), grammarian and ethnographer, 'one of the finest brains of modern times'. They seem to have met at Lamalou, where Brachet was taking the waters 'for neuralgic pains', according to Léon Daudet.

The little chap with St Vitus's dance; his convulsive movements. Terrible to watch. Can't speak anymore. Father, mother, grandmother, sister.

The man who drove the Tsar's train along a stretch of track the Nihilists had reportedly mined. A twenty-minute journey, at the end of which the illness declared itself: pain in the eyes, then blindness.

That child's arm: no more than an ivory scratching hand at the end of a mahogany ruler.

The blind Russian, talking about the clinic in the rue Visconti. He was put in a large room with people he didn't know, who kept changing, whom he never saw, and who never saw him.

Major B—— confides in me.

His farewell to the regiment; last dinner in the mess. Sold his last horse. Varying state of his blindness. Days when, as he puts it, 'Everything's black . . . quite black . . .' Then he's afraid. Other times, there's a break in the clouds. His delight when they take him to rehearsals. 'She's the leading singer!' Memories of garrison life. The servant who looked after them. Very chic.

And like the blind man, I too say, 'Everything's black . . . quite black . . .' This is the colour of my whole life nowadays.

In the Land of Pain

Pain blots out the horizon, fills everything.

I've passed the stage where illness brings any advantage, or helps you understand things; also the stage where it sours your life, puts a harshness in your voice, makes every cog-wheel shriek.

Now there's only a hard, stagnant, painful torpor, and an indifference to everything. *Nada! . . . Nada! . . .*

The mysteries of female illness; clitoral maladies. The woman of sixty who fainted clean away.

Women's heroism in the face of their ills.

I think about the nervous anxiety which must run through mills and brothels and places where large numbers of women exist in close proximity, during those periods when they are all shaken according to their different temperaments.

Monsieur C——, who lives with a noise perpetually in his head, like the whistle of a locomotive, or rather, like steam escaping. You can get used to anything.

The joy of an ataxic who notices an improvement in his condition. The man with suddenly shining eyes.

The officer who lost all power of speech after falling

from his horse. Just a few words in a shaky voice. Looks like a Swede.

Among the patients, the young polyglot Spaniard; memories of his earliest childhood have resurfaced, including the patois of the Balearic Islands, where he'd been put out to nurse and then stayed until he was five.*

Only at Lamalou have I seen wives keeping such a close watch on their husbands, preventing people from talking

---

* According to Goncourt (12 January 1896), the sudden patois-speaker was the same person as the officer who fell off his horse in the preceding entry. According to Léon Daudet (*Devant la Douleur*), he was the same person as the Russian train-driver who passed from apparent health to advanced ataxia in twenty minutes (p. 64); and *he* was the same as Major B—— (p. 64) who suffered varying states of blindness. Léon Daudet particularizes them: a 'white' blindness, which was more or less bearable, and a 'black' version which induced thoughts of suicide. Blindness was a feature of advanced tertiary syphilis (see the case of Xavier Aubryet, pp. 34–5).

Such textual disparities in ataxia case-history might be partly cleared up if the manuscript of *La Doulou* were available for examination. It is currently untraceable, having apparently been dispersed, along with other notebooks, after Lucien Daudet's death in 1946. The text was certainly edited before first publication; how much was cut or rearranged is impossible to guess.

to them, so that they don't discover anything about their illness.

The Russian who can't move his arms and has a servant to roll cigarettes for him. They have a row: the servant has to make furious gestures for both of them.

Old, sapless fruit-trees, as lopsided as ataxics: Lamalou.

The hotel. The bell-board. The bath times.
Solitude.
Encroaching darkness.

Coming back again and again to the same place, like the wall you stood against as a child and on which they marked your height. A quantifiable change every time. But whereas the marks on the wall always demonstrated growth, now there is only regression and diminution.

This year, at Lamalou, there are stairs I can't get down any more. Putting one foot in front of another is dreadful. Going for a walk is impossible. I am too indolent to get up. In bed my legs are made of stone which feels pain.

The man who watches the others suffer.
The doppelgangers.

The street, carriages passing at a gallop.
Lamalou in winter.
'In the land of pain.'

Doctors are building themselves houses at Lamalou.
They have such faith! — and such big black hats!

The Russian who actually prefers just to suffer. How I
understand what he said to me yesterday: 'Pain stops me
from thinking.'

One of the blind patients at Lamalou has come from
the depths of Japan; his groping journey here. The sounds
of the sea, of towns, of steamers . . .*

* Daudet was so myopic that he once talked for a quarter of an
hour to a rug thrown over a chair, in the belief that it was Edmond
de Goncourt. He would have imagined the voyage well. 'This
evening Daudet talked passionately about the sea. He said that
he didn't experience its magic through those colours which painters
apprehend, but, thanks to an extraordinarily well-calibrated ear,
through its musical aspects: its distant lamentations, the roar as
it breaks against the rocks, and the sound of wet flapping sheets
that it makes on the shore. Then he imitated its sounds.'
(Goncourt, 22 November 1891). Léon Daudet, on the other hand,
says that his father 'perceived colour and form with the greatest
liveliness' and was 'one of the very first to appreciate the
Impressionists'.

In the Land of Pain

The family pool, where I prefer to bathe, usually alone, has a sinister look to it. You go down a few steps. It's four or five metres square, like one of the Inquisition's dungeons. Roughcast walls, light coming from a large skylight high overhead. Running round the inside of the bath is a stone bench, invisible because of the opaqueness of the yellow water.

I sit there by myself with my copy of Montaigne, my constant companion; iron, sulphur and the waters of every spa have left their various traces on the book, their alluvial deposits. A large curtain covers the entrance and hides me from the female bathers who are walking past or being dried in front of the fire. All the time there are people chatting away; often they're locals from the Midi, telling one another what they've been up to.

People are just as open and expansive as anywhere else. News and gossip about the different hotels, with everyone ridiculously proud of the one they happen to be staying at. Disagreements about the temperature of the water; each bather seems to have his own fantasy thermometer. Conversations overheard from neighbouring pools. People recognizing one another, catching up on the last twelve months' news, and so on.

I've overheard people talking about me, sometimes maliciously, sometimes sympathetically. I also eavesdrop on the chaps who work here, boisterous Cévennes peasants who speak patois; they are honest, intelligent, sturdy, prudent and sly. One of them has worked here for forty years.

The footfall of ataxics; the sound of sticks and crutches; occasionally the noise of someone falling over. Exchange between two servants (in patois): 'What's that?' 'Nothing . . . the old geezer's just bloody fallen over again.'

A sudden, mysterious drama in the pool. A terrified voice calling the attendant: 'Chéron! Quick! (*a crescendo of fear*) Quick! Quick!' Then everyone together, voices filled with panic: 'Colard, Chéron! Quick! Quick!'

Among the ladies. A dear old nun. 'Haven't had a bath for fifty years,' she says as she comes in.

Russians, both men and women, go into the baths naked. No diseases to hide! Alarm among the Southerners.

The old Priapus, soaked in laudanum. With others, it's more a question of lost virility.

This year I've met a lot of people with double vision,* and diseases of the eye.

* 'Daudet complains that in literary matters he always has two different ideas about the same subject, and the struggle in his head between these two ideas makes work difficult, hesitant and confused. He calls this his *double vision*. He says that when he

Sick children.

Talked to one of them. A certain pride about the pain he suffers. (Fragility of the bones.)

S—— B——. These strange seasons here.

Sexual fantasies, of a cerebral kind.

A couple of old ataxics playing cards, and picking up by old women who take them off to a distant villa. Later, the two men on crutches returning secretively late at night by a back route.

Some exotic patients, like big black flies.

The campaigns of Baron X——, an old voluptuary now a little soft in the head. When he was fifteen, his uncle the Marquis de Z—— took him to dinner at the Café Anglais. The events of that evening resulted in a travel warrant for Lamalou. But he's not in any pain. Elegant and empty-headed,

———

suffered his first great attack, he used to laugh at seeing two milestones or two fountains by the side of the road, when there was only one milestone and one fountain; and that this double vision of his has now turned into the double thought of which he now complains.' (Goncourt, 3 February 1889) he tells stories of high society. Goes to mass with his man-servant.

X——, driven mad with pain. Two hundred drops of laudanum per day. A figure in a long frock coat, making expansive gestures.

Major Z——. During a dance lesson the poor blind fellow starts shouting at the ataxics, 'Take your places for the pastourelle!' Looking like an imbecile in the middle of the drawing room.

Old man C—— outside the hotel. He no longer takes the waters but comes here just to look at the ataxics.

A doctor told me that in the Catholic South a lot of the women he examines are so embarrassed that when he asks them a question about their illness, they reply, 'Yes, Father . . .'

Racehorses given morphine injections to stop them winning the cup.

A striking account from the pool attendant of how they subdued the madman. They seized hold of him, threw him on the bed and held him down until the houseman came running and gave him one, two, three injections in succession – enough to stun an ox. That quietened him down a bit.

In the Land of Pain

At the start of each season at Lamalou the patients, in all their weirdness and diversity, draw comfort from the demonstration that their respective illnesses all have something in common.

Then, when the season's over and the baths close, this whole agglomeration of pain breaks up and disperses. Each of these patients turns back into a loner, someone isolated and lost amid the noise and turbulence of life, just a strange creature with a funny illness, almost certainly a hypochondriac, whom one has to feel sorry for but who is really rather boring.

Only at Lamalou is he understood, only there are people truly interested in his disease.

The torment of coming back to the same spot again: 'I used to do that ... I used to be able to do this ... Well, now I can't anymore.'

Lamalou is showing a new face this year. They play a South American waltz, 'La Rosita'. The Brazilian sitting in his chair; sallow complexion and look of despair.

The attitude of priests to pain and suffering.*

---

* 'There were ataxic priests there who of course never used morphine, and endured extraordinary suffering in a Christian manner; whereas doctors, on the whole, as soon as the first

The little Benedictine monk, detached from everything.

The walks I used to take around this land of pain. Could still find it in myself to laugh. Lunches. La Bellocquière. Seen it all again in my mind's eye. Villemagne and the Pont-du-Diable. Felt like crying. I remember what Caoudal said: 'And to think that I shall come to regret all this!'*

All those huntsmen in the Midi get rheumatism from shooting scoter-duck in the marshes. Some of them come here for preventative treatment.

The new pool. So why spend four years in the old one?

The small boy carried into the pool with his toy boat.

One ought to go to different baths each season.

I've come to understand the panicky indecision of some

---

symptoms declared themselves, turned straightaway to calming poisons'. (Léon Daudet, *Devant la Douleur*)

* Caoudal is the sculptor in Daudet's novel *Sapho* (1884); after being abandoned by a young mistress, he utters these words 'with the foresight of the ageing dandy mourning his decay'. According to Léon Daudet, Caoudal was based on the photographer Nadar.

poor piece of human wreckage in the pool. Also the sad little cry of 'Wait while I check' from some poor wretch feeling to see if his legs are still there.

Exchange between the bachelor and the married man. The problem of jealousy, when a man is no longer a man and becomes unable to defend his hearth and home.

On the hotel terrace, the to-and-fro of the sick, of invalid carriages and patients with their companions.

A family goes by, the father leaning on his daughter, the mother following with an embarrassed small boy. Comments: 'That poor fellow's really ill.' 'Yes, but look how his family cares for him and loves him . . .'

The sight of this family yesterday gave me the idea for a dramatic dialogue which would be worth developing.

FIRST ATAXIC *(with that hypocritical commiseration which fails to disguise the satisfaction a sick person feels on seeing someone sicker than himself):* That poor old fellow looks really ill.

SECOND ATAXIC *(a small man, gnarled as a vine, in such pain that the slightest movement makes him cry out):* You don't need to feel sorry for him — he's well looked after, he's pampered . . . His wife, his children — look at that pretty, grown-up daughter, oozing tender concern at every step.

Look how she watches over his every need, and sees that nothing happens to him. *I* live with just a servant who's never there, who parks me in the sitting room like a broom and forgets about me, who watches me suffer with either indifference or a feigned sympathy which I find even more loathsome.

FIRST ATAXIC: You don't know your luck! I know what it is to be ill in the bosom of your family, I can tell you about that. Unless you want to behave like an abominable egotist, you have to avoid giving expression to your pain so as not to upset those around you. If you've got small children, you don't want to spoil the few happy, innocent hours of their lives, leaving them with the memory of an old dad who was always moaning and complaining. It's a terrible weight on a household, having someone around like us, someone whose illness drags on for years and years . . . It's perfectly obvious from the way *you* writhe about and complain all the time that you live by yourself. You're allowed to suffer without embarrassment or constraint.

SECOND ATAXIC: You'll be saying next that when someone's in pain they don't have the right to mention it!

FIRST ATAXIC: But I'm in pain too, at this very moment. It's just that I've trained myself to keep my suffering to myself. When the pain gets so bad that I have to give vent to it, you should see the fuss it causes! 'What's the matter? Where does it hurt?' I have to admit that 'what's the matter' is always the same, and that they'd be perfectly justified in replying, 'Oh, if that's all it is.' Our pain is always new to us, but becomes quite familiar to those around us. It soon wears out its welcome, even for those who love us the most. Compassion loses its edge. Even if I didn't try to keep my suffering to myself out of concern for others, I would do so out of pride: I don't want to read weariness and boredom in the eyes of those dearest to me. And then, if you live by yourself, you don't have the endless anxieties of the family man: sick children, bringing them up properly, education, maintaining your authority as a father, taking care of a wife you have no right to turn into a home nurse. And there's the hearth you can't defend, that you're no longer in any condition to defend . . . No, the only real way to be ill is to be by yourself.

The bachelor would then cite all the anguish that he has to keep to himself and is unable to share, the lack of love and affection, etc., and would conclude that it is the very responsibilities of the family man which often serve to reduce the level of his suffering.

———————————

The text of *La Doulou* breaks off here. According to André Ebner, Daudet stopped taking notes for it about three years before his death. This is an approximation: one note — concerning the Daudets' visit to Venice — can clearly be dated to eighteen months before the writer's death. Ebner also wrote of those final years: 'His passion for his work, for the discussion of ideas, and his desire to read something new every day (towards the end he was keenly devouring the most difficult scientific texts) were stronger than his illness. He stopped examining it, and transformed his unceasing torments into a goodness which increased with each day.' Ebner quotes him from this time as wanting to be 'nothing more than a vendor of happiness'.

He was already that. Daudet presents himself at Lamalou as an interested, sometimes pitiless, observer and overhearer. His son Léon, who accompanied him there in 1885 and 1887, saw him in more active, public, philanthropic mode. Daudet was a star patient, and his arrival at the Hôtel Mas one of the events of the season. 'From the first evening,' Léon remembered, 'we would be surrounded by about sixty people, familiar faces smiling at us through their torments. It was the most extraordinary display of moral attraction I have ever been permitted to witness.' As well as resident sage and moral guide, Daudet was an after-dinner act — reading and commenting on Montaigne and Rabelais — and cheerleader on picnics in the surrounding countryside. Lunches would be provided by Mme Mas, and for a few hours muscular atrophy, ataxia and aphasia were forgotten as 'this troupe of involuntary tragedians allowed themselves to play comedy'. Not that tragedy was ever far away. Doctors were always at hand in case of what were referred to as 'accidents'. Léon recounts a typical 'accident': a paralytic in the bath asks his neighbour politely, 'Excuse me, Sir, but is this leg yours or mine?' 'Yours, I believe,' comes the answer, at which the paralytic falls backwards and dies.

Daudet's advice to his fellow-patients was pragmatic. Illness should be treated as an unwanted guest, to whom no special attention is accorded; daily life should continue as normally as possible. 'I don't believe I will get better,' he said, 'and nor does Charcot. Yet I always behave as if my damned pains were going to disappear by tomorrow morning.' Léon Daudet recalled his father

seated in the little garden of the Hôtel Mas at Lamalou surrounded by sick people, preaching energy to them, reassuring the nervous ones, taking pains with the despairing, and giving them glimpses of some possible holding-off or drawing-back of their fate: 'The doctors don't know any more than we do; in fact they know even less, because their knowledge is made up of an average drawn from observations which are generally hasty and incomplete, and because every case is a new and particular one. You,

Sir, have this symptom, and you over there have another. It would be necessary to join you both to Madame here in order to obtain something which resembles somewhat my own martyrdom. There are a great many different kinds of instrument belonging to the executioner; if they do not scare you too much, examine them carefully. It is with our torments as it is with shadows. Attention clears them up and drives them away.'

Daudet knew, however, that some torments could not be driven away by intellectual examination. His greatest fear was that he would eventually descend into total paralysis, aphasia and imbecility: what he refers to in *La Doulou* as an *in pace*, a living tomb. This at least he was spared. In October 1897 the family moved to 41, rue de l'Université (Goncourt noted that whenever his friend changed apartments, his first, ritual action was to look for where his coffin was likely to rest). On 16 December Daudet worked on the dramatization of his novel *La Petite Paroisse*, then sat down to dinner with his wife, three children and mother-in-law. He seemed in good spirits. He took a few spoonfuls of soup, and was chatting away about Edmond Rostand, whose play *Cyrano de Bergerac* was just going into general rehearsal. Suddenly, in Léon Daudet's account, the family heard 'that frightful noise which one never forgets – a veiled rattle in the throat followed by another rattle'. The vendor of happiness fell back in his chair and died.

As an ending this is neat, and a little novelistic. The filial version shirks the kind of detail the father liked to note. In its issue of 1 January 1898, *La Chronique médicale* reported that when Daudet collapsed two doctors were called: Dr Gilles de la Tourette (after whom Tourette's syndrome was named) and Daudet's old friend Dr Potain. They first checked for food lodged in the throat, and then 'for an hour and a half' gave artificial respiration by the bizarre and briefly fashionable method of 'rhythmical tractions of the tongue' (an 1892 paper had recommended forceful and persistent pulling on the tongue in cases of asphyxia by sewer-gas). When this failed the doctors tried 'faradization of the diaphragm' — stimulating the diaphragmatic muscle with alternating current. Only afterwards did they pronounce Daudet to be dead.

Edmond de Goncourt had died the previous year, at Champrosay, thus confirming his generous contention that his friend would outlive him. Daudet 'received his last sigh', as the French say. Mme Daudet would live on another four decades, long enough to bury her own daughter, Edmée, the child of Lamalou. She authorized the publication of *La Doulou* in 1930, and herself died in 1940, the centenary of Daudet's birth.

A Note on Syphilis

The return of Columbus and his crew from the Americas in 1493 set off a pandemic of syphilis throughout Europe. After nearly three centuries of routine destructiveness, the disease came up with two new transformations in the late eighteenth century. Both involved the disease moving, in its tertiary stage, into the nervous system: general paresis (also known as general paralysis of the insane, GPI) and tabes dorsalis, usually shortened to tabes. Perhaps five to seven percent of men who caught syphilis developed GPI or tabes; the figure for women was much lower.

Tabes normally began to manifest itself fifteen to thirty-five years after initial infection. One of its primary clinical features was 'lightning pains' — sharp, stabbing, intense and repetitive. They varied from the mild, when they might be given the folk diagnosis of 'rheumatism', to 'one of the most agonizing known to medicine'. A current handbook of clinical neurology states simply: 'The pain is often so intolerable as to make the patient contemplate suicide.'

Daudet remarks early on in *La Doulou* that the disease was 'sounding me out, choosing its ground'. In fact, it would choose many grounds at the same time: there could be gastric and laryngeal crises, bone problems, rectal and urinary crises (hence his consultation with Dr Guyon). Further, there were sensory disruptions: from numbness of the feet to 'girdle pains' – a sense of having a tight band round the upper abdomen, which Daudet describes as the 'breastplate' he is unable to remove. The first study of *La Doulou* from a medical point of view, Mary Trivas's *Auto-observation d'un tabétique de qualité* (1932), judged that its opening pages constituted 'a complete symptomological list of pre-ataxic tabes'; the case was more than 'classic', it was '*livresque*' – textbook.

The ataxic period proper declared itself with unsteadiness in walking, a deficiency at first compensated for by the visual sense (hence Daudet's note about being able to walk better if he could see his shadow). Tabetics were more unsteady in the dark and – as Romberg's test (1846) showed – would often fall over if they closed their eyes. Lack of control over the legs could be accompanied by lack of feeling for them: the classic ataxic, wrote Trivas, would complain of 'losing his legs in the bed' (Daudet: 'my legs get confused'). Then progressive paralysis would ensue. Arms and hands were also affected: Mme Daudet noted early on that her husband's 'fine, clear' handwriting had begun to show 'a light tremble'.

The historian Augustin Thierry (1795–1856), one of the first tabetics to describe the condition from the inside, said that you were resigned 'to seeing yourself disappear piece by piece'. Sensory, muscular, visceral and motor problems developed; although normally no ataxic developed all the symptoms of tabes. Daudet, for instance, escaped blindness (though he suffered visual disruptions), and also, in Trivas's judgement, 'the gastric crises of tabes'. Visceral torments are certainly mentioned in *La Doulou;* but they were more likely the consequence of using morphine and other painkillers. Similarly, when Daudet describes how various forms of hand-writing dance before his eyes, Trivas finds such '*mentisme*' a classic hallucinatory effect of opium and its derivatives, one similar to the 'visual drunkenness' induced by peyote.

If the tabetic could not always be sure if his suffering was caused by his illness or its treatment (or palliation), it was also unclear to many what had caused the condition. Given the time-gap between initial infection and tertiary neurosyphilis, the connection was for long not apparent. Duchenne de Boulogne is generally credited with first insisting on the causal link between syphilis and locomotor ataxia; Alfred Fournier confirmed it statistically, and began to teach that view from about 1880. But conventional medical opinion was conservative and unconvinced for many years. Charcot, who dealt with the most influential patients of the day, rejected the connection right up until his death in 1893. Daudet was treated by Fournier as well as by Charcot, and privately agreed with Fournier's conclusions.

A Note on Syphilis

The patient's moral and psychological response to his condition also varied. Anatole France quoted Daudet as saying, shortly before his death, 'I am justly punished for having loved life too much'; but this sounds altogether too pat. The text of *La Doulou* contains anguished regret for the loss of faculties and the infliction of suffering on others, but never descends into moralizing. In any case, attitudes to the acquisition of syphilis were more complicated than we might imagine. For some it was a badge of manhood, proof of sexual bravado; there was even a belief that it brought enhanced creative and imaginative powers. Baudelaire said that a young writer correcting his proofs for the first time was 'as proud as a schoolboy getting his first dose of the pox'. And when Maupassant started treatment for syphilis in 1877, he was exultant: 'My hair is beginning to grow again and the hair on my arse is sprouting. I've got the pox! At last! Not the contemptible clap ... no, no, the great pox, the one François I died of. The majestic pox ... and I'm proud of it, by thunder. I don't have to worry about catching it any more, and I screw the street whores and trollops, and afterwards say to them, "I've got the pox."' Maupassant subsequently developed GPI, attempted suicide in 1891, and died, after eighteen months in a lunatic asylum, in 1893.

Mercury was widely used to treat syphilis during much of the nineteenth century, giving rise to the joke about 'spending one night with Venus and the rest of your life with Mercury'. Daudet consulted all the greatest specialists of his day, and tried all their treatments, from the gentlest to the most outlandish; nothing slowed, or even much alleviated, the course of his disease. (The Seyre suspension, incidentally, crossed the Atlantic. In April 1890 Dr S. Weir Mitchell reported in the *University Medical Magazine* his use of an apparatus which was 'a modification of the suspension arrangement of Dr Motchoukowsky, of Odessa'. Mitchell's improvement was to suspend the patient by the elbows as well as the chin and occiput, thus greatly reducing the pain while still stretching the spinal cord. He hung up twenty-three of his patients, a number of them ataxic, for as many as fifty times, and some dutifully declared 'a certain indescribable sense of gain'.)

Statistics for the prevalence of syphilis in the nineteenth century are inherently unreliable. Flaubert's sardonic entry in his *Dictionary of Accepted Ideas* reads: 'Syphilis: everyone, more or less, suffers from it.' Some detect a general decline from the 1860s; all that seems certain is that the disease tended to flourish best during and after times of war (Napoleonic, First World), and during large movements of population. Effective identification and treatment of syphilis only arrived in the twentieth century. The Wassermann serological test came into use in 1906; Salvarsan, an arsenic compound which worked successfully against primary and secondary infections, was patented in 1909; penicillin, discovered in 1928, was first used against syphilis by Mahoney in 1943. Since then, the prevalence of the disease has been greatly reduced.

I recently discussed Daudet's case with a friend who is a specialist in sexually transmitted diseases. 'Syphilis has become boring since penicillin,' he told me. (Boring for the doctor, anyway.) Though the disease has been more or less eradicated domestically, mass air travel still brings him a few cases. A couple of years ago he treated a group of young men who all appeared to have something in common – apart from their infection, that is. They were, it turned out, England football supporters who had followed the national team to a friendly game in Moldova, and had been impressed by how much extra friendliness their money had bought. If any of them were to read *La Doulou*, they might realize how great their historical luck had been.

J. B.

Alphonse Daudet was born in Nîmes, France, in 1840. Novelist, play-wright and journalist, his success came through his novels and stories. He contracted syphilis at the age of seventeen and died at the age of fifty-seven.

Julian Barnes is the author of nine novels, a book of stories, and a collection of essays. He is the recipient of the Prix Femina and in 1988 was made an *Officier de l'Ordre des Arts et des Lettres.* He lives in London.

A Note on the Type

The text of this book was set in Centaur, the only typeface designed by Bruce Rogers (1870–1957), the well-known American book designer. A celebrated penman, Rogers based his design on the roman face cut by Nicolas Jenson in 1470 for his Eusebius. Jenson's roman surpassed all of its forerunners and even today, in modern recuttings, remains one of the most popular and attractive of all typefaces. The italic used to accompany Centaur is Arrighi, designed by another American, Frederic Warde, and based on the chancery face used by Lodovico degli Arrighi in 1524.

Composed by North Market Street Graphics,
Lancaster, Pennsylvania

Printed and bound by R.R. Donnelley & Sons
Harrisonburg, Virginia